Toddler
Owner's
Manual

For my darling Zara and Eloise, one of you has finished toddling and the other is about to start. Thank you for the love and laughter and constant inspiration, and more than anything, thank you to my beautiful wife Elana, whose constant support and encouragement gets me off my behind and writing. I love you all.

Toddler Owner's Manual
Father's Edition

Steve Bedwell

A Rockpool book

PO Box 252
Summer Hill
NSW 2130

www.rockpoolpublishing.com.au

First published in 2014

National Library of Australia Cataloguing-in-Publication entry

Bedwell, Steve, author.

Toddler owner's manual / Steve Bedwell.

Father's edition

9781925017199 (paperback)
Infants--Care.
Fatherhood.
649.122

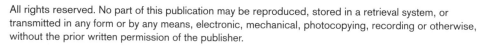

Edited by Glenda Downing
Cover and internal design by Debaser
Picture research by Emelie Ousback
Typeset by TypeSkill
All images sourced from Shutterstock
Printed and bound in India
10 9 8 7 6 5 4 3 2 1

Contents

A word of introduction from Mother Nature Heavy Industries Pty Ltd

Congratulations, your Mother Nature Heavy Industries (MNHI) baby is no longer a baby, he has entered the second stage of his development and, as a result, the second stage of your ownership. Your baby is now officially a toddler. MNHI officially describes a toddler as being in that stage after infancy and before childhood, predominantly between the ages of 12 to 36 months when the child begins to walk unsteadily or 'toddle'.

MNHI wishes to remind you that your child is no longer covered by the MNHI 12-month unlimited kilometre crawling warranty and, as such, the father is liable for any servicing or extra attention the toddler may need during this precarious period. Additional warranty protection can be purchased from your local MNHI dealer, the cost of which may vary depending upon the intended usage of the toddler and where the toddler will be housed. Additional warranty protection is advised particularly in the case of more rambunctious and accident-prone boy model toddlers.

This is also a stage of great development in other areas of your child's life, as he grows into a period known as 'the terrible twos'. Your toddler will at various

times be unpredictable, destructive and above all, demanding. MNHI has designed this manual as a survival guide for fathers as they steer a course through this most testing of times in their child's growth.

This MNHI manual will cover all aspects of toddler ownership. It is important to note that although your toddler may be out of the official MNHI warranty period, full servicing and maintenance enquiries can be handled at additional cost by any one of the 211 MNHI service centres nation wide. It is strongly recommended that any repairs or maintenance required by your toddler be carried out at one of these authorised service centres to maintain the integrity of your toddler's operating systems.

As with the *Baby Owner's Manual*, the *Toddler Owner's Manual* is designed to enable fathers to navigate this most challenging of periods by empowering them with the prerequisite skills and knowledge to match their child's developmental stage. Toddlers grow and

develop at different rates and, accordingly, this manual is purely a guide as to what a father can expect during the 24-month toddler period. Fathers should not be alarmed if their child does not begin walking until 24 months, as every child MNHI produces is individually programmed to meet different performance goals.

The problems faced by the owner of a toddler are many and varied, from tantrums and the eruption of teeth to confronting the use of the toilet for the first time, from eating to sleeping and every developmental stage in between. MNHI trained professionals are here to help at every step of the way.

The toddler stage is full of joy and changes, and although at times these challenges may seem insurmountable, this manual and the advice contained within will steer any father through the turbulent times that lie ahead. As such, MNHI suggests that you take time to fully absorb this manual and follow the recommendations contained within.

MNHI has taken great care and consideration in compiling this manual to ensure your every query is met in a way that will not only provide peace of mind but also simplicity and clarity of purpose for the efficient and trouble-free ownership and operation of your toddler. As a result of years of research and development, this manual has been divided into the following five easy-to-read, understand and implement sections:

Section A: The Road to Toddling This section will deal with the period of ownership up until your toddler's first steps, including the celebration of the completion of the first year of ownership and suggestions for how to commemorate this event. This event is of great significance to the owner and co-owner, even though your toddler will remember nothing of it.

Section B: The Terrible Twos The 'terrible twos' is defined as that period of toddler ownership that can range between 18 and 30 months, and is widely acknowledged as the most problematic time faced by the father and co-owner as the toddler becomes more aware and mobile. This section will help the father navigate this most testing of periods and the inevitable tantrums that follow.

Section C: Eating, Sleeping and Toilet Training Now that your child is at the toddler stage its requirements for fuel and waste disposal will alter dramatically from

when it was a baby. This section will school the father in the changing dietary and toilet habits of the toddler, as well as how to smoothly implement them.

Section D: Correcting Bad Habits and Unwanted Behaviour
As toddlers develop so does their desire to misbehave or 'breakdown'. This section will highlight some of the more destructive and antisocial behaviours of the toddler and advise how the father can take corrective measures for his own sanity to prevent these from occurring in the future.

Section E: Entertainment and Beyond the Home
During this growth period of 12 to 36 months your toddler's entertainment needs will develop exponentially. You will also need to spend time away from

your toddler to conduct your life. This section deals with keeping your toddler busy as well as discussing alternative care scenarios.

Finally, MNHI would like to take this opportunity to congratulate fathers on their child making the transition from baby to toddler. We emphasis, it is a testing time of ownership but rest assured, MNHI will continue to show interest and render assistance to ensure your parenting pleasure and satisfaction. By using the information contained in this manual and by seeking the assistance of MNHI professionals where required, satisfactory toddler operation and a fulfilling ownership experience can be achieved.

The information provided in this manual was correct at the time of printing. Evolutionary advances and social circumstances mean that MNHI may change the contents of this manual and toddler specifications without notice and without incurring obligation.

Section A:
The Road to Toddling

The First Anniversary

The first year of ownership of your child has been a tough one with many compromises to you and the co-owner's lifestyle and habits, not to mention sleep deprivation. Let's face it, babies and their nocturnal habits can be a nightmare. MNHI deliberately engineers its babies this way to prepare you for the rigors of toddler ownership.

how to mark this momentous occasion. This occasion and the ensuing event will be henceforth be referred to as 'the party'.

The end of warranty party is a time of great rejoicing for the owner and co-owner. Suddenly your baby is not a baby any more and the security of the MNHI warranty protection plan has passed. What better time to celebrate…or perhaps not? For the sake of the party and the enjoyment of the invitees, MNHI suggests that you concentrate on the birthday and less on the warranty running out.

Successfully raising a baby and getting to the end of the warranty period and to the commencement of the toddler phase of your child's life is an event to be celebrated, and MNHI has several recommendations on

MNHI would like to address several of the more common questions that its consultants get asked in relation to the one-year birthday party.

Who should I invite? MNHI advises it is important that this milestone be shared with as many of your living relatives as possible, even though you might not have seen most of them since you first took delivery of the

baby. This is so you don't have to see the annoying ones for at least another year, and also to increase the present haul.

An array of adult friends should also be invited to the party. These are those friends who have been there for you with advice and assistance, whether wanted or not – let's face it, everyone's an expert – during the hiccups of the first year of ownership. This, too, will also help to increase the present haul.

It is important to point out that one of the prime reasons for hosting a first birthday party is the presents…it's not like the child is going to remember it. Those adult friends you invite may also have children of a similar age, so you will be able compare the progress of your child with theirs. When comparing children and their progress, it is important to exaggerate and paint your child as being far more advanced than he is, because if you don't, the other parents will beat you to it.

Feel free to also invite acquaintances you have met during the course of your first year of baby ownership. You may have met these people through parent support groups or at a MNHI service centre while your babies were being attended to. Once again, these guests will bring presents for your child, and this is primarily what the party is about.

Remember, this is a baby party in name alone. This event is actually an excuse to get adults together to socialise and compare notes on toddler ownership. It should be noted that at least half of the advice given by friends and relatives on toddler-raising should be discarded as inaccurate or out-and-out lies. The correct and most up-to-date guide to owning, operating and maintaining a toddler is contained within this manual.

The baby component of the party should be kept to a minimum, apart from the prerequisite handing the baby around from excited person to excited person, like some human pass the parcel. Although you may not enjoy relinquishing your baby to all and sundry, MNHI has carefully designed its babies to absorb this kind of treatment. From sloppy kisses to an accidental extension of the neck, rest assured your baby is hardy and resilient to all that excited adults can subject it to.

It is the adults that make the one-year birthday party fun, so choose your guests wisely. Avoid heavy drinkers, smokers and especially the clumsy as there will be lots of little hands and feet to be trodden on if not careful.

Where and when should I hold the party? The ideal setting for a one-year party is the home. A familiar environment is essential for the comfort and convenience of the pre-toddler and their owners. The birthday boy or girl will be blissfully unaware they are the centre of attention and will still need to stick to their prescribed eating and sleeping regime. Also, should the father and co-owner decide to have a celebratory drink, having the party at home negates the need to make alternative transportation arrangements.

recommends that the father and co-owner do have a drink at the one-year birthday celebration as this may be the last time you can put your baby down and know that he will be where you left him when you come back. Soon he will be a toddler and the life of doing what you want when you want will be over.

Try to plan the timing of the party around the sleep cycle of the child to ensure the majority of the party takes place during the child's waking hours. Nobody wants to come and celebrate with a sleeping guest of honour, unless of course the party is for a 90 year old, in which case the preferable time to celebrate is while they are sleeping.

MNHI can also host a one-year birthday party at any of its service centres. Our trained party planners and technicians can cater for all the needs of your end-of-warranty function while at the same time carrying out a final inspection on the child to cover off any existing issues before the warranty expires.

What presents can I expect? It is the experience of MNHI that the majority of presents for a one year old will be inappropriate or unusable in the short term. Books seem to be popular gifts, for some reason. The child has yet to develop the fine motor skills to hold a book much less be able to read, rendering books useless. Shoes are also a popular

if nonsensical gift. Although the child will soon be toddling, at this stage he tends to do a lot of lying around, for which shoes are not really necessary. MNHI suggests, and there is a gift register facility at all of our service centres, that toys which increase hand–eye coordination and have a relaxing musical component are ideal presents. The gift registry is the suggested route to take as history tells us that people really don't think about the gifts they buy a one year old and often give things that represent a choking hazard.

What about food and cake? Once again it is important to remember that this is a child's party in name alone, and the food on offer should reflect this. Bearing in mind that most of the guest of honour's contemporaries are either still on formula or eating mush, a barbecue is the perfect catering solution, with steak and sausages covering all the needs of both the adults and the older children. A cursory nod can be given to the more youthful party attendees by placing bowls of mixed sweets around the house.

A wide selection of alcoholic beverages should be available for the adults, both for general consumption and toasting the birthday child. Keep in mind this will be your last chance to cater a birthday party to suit yourself. By the time your toddler hits the second birthday, the party will suddenly be all about him and what he wants to eat and drink…and that's even before you get into the sketchy world of children's entertainment.

The end-of-warranty or first birthday celebrations are traditionally capped off with a cake. As with all facets of the party, the cake should be approached primarily with the adults in mind. It should be adult in flavour – black forest or carrot, for example – but child-like in design, say a cartoon character. The cartoon character is there for the photographic record of the day and candle blowing purposes, whereas the flavour is purely for the enjoyment of the adult attendees. MNHI suggests that all cakes be nut free. Although all MNHI babies are produced with a high allergenic tolerance, these tolerances can reduce with age.

MNHI congratulates you on reaching this milestone and wishes you well with your first birthday/

end-of-warranty party and looks forward to being of assistance in the next phase of toddler ownership.

First Steps

Now that your baby has reached one year of age, some remarkable things begin to happen. These changes may occur anytime between 12 and 18 months and will involve the child slowly gaining independent mobility, or toddling. At the end of the first year your baby will have mastered crawling, but it is important to note that MNHI programs its babies to develop at different rates when it comes to the major motor skills (walking, running, climbing etc.). It is also important to note that when it comes to walking, late developers tend to catch up very quickly, so that by 24 months all MNHI babies are at approximately the same stage of walking development and mobility. They will all be at the same stage of developing their destructive powers as well.

Once toddling has commenced (and it will happen in the blink of an eye) you will find that your life as an owner will be very different. A mobile toddler is a busy and inquisitive toddler, and he will be into everything before you notice it. You must never take your eye off a toddler because he will be out of the house and halfway down the street before you realise it. One minute it is those first tentative steps, the next it is climbing stairs and running. If you have a dog or cat, your pet can expect a whole new world of tail-pulling and general interference with its daily routine from your now mobile toddler. From 12 months on, MNHI suggests that you have a video camera or smartphone on hand at all times in anticipation of the all-important walking milestone. Always be prepared. Should you as the owner miss recording those precious first steps you will never hear the end of it from the co-owner.

MNHI also manufactures a range of walking aids to help your child's balance and build confidence in those first tentative steps as he gains mobility. These aids are modelled on a frame on wheels, and are manufactured in different colours and fitted with accessories to amuse your toddler. Please note that these frames are specifically tailored to toddlers and under no circumstances should an elderly relative's Zimmer frame be modified for child use.

It will take plenty of practice for your toddler to reach full confidence in movement, and MNHI urges you to encourage him at every step to accelerate this development, even though your instincts may tell you to keep him immobile for as long as possible. There will be tumbles, falls and tears, but MNHI assures owners that this is normal and serious injuries requiring a trip to the service centre are rare. What follows is the MNHI guide to toddler development and what you can expect.

12 to 15 Months Some 12 month olds are already walking by themselves, and some may have already been at it for a while. Others are just beginning to pull themselves up to standing, and still others may have been standing for a while but are yet to take those first tentative unassisted steps. By the time they reach 15 months the vast majority of toddlers who haven't begun to walk by themselves will be engaging in what is known as cruising. Cruising is the stage of development whereby the toddler is taking a few cautious steps while holding onto furniture, your hands or a MNHI-approved walking frame or push toy. Cruising is also known in parenting circles as the calm before the storm.

15 to 18 Months By 15 months the early walkers are probably already highly skilled in the art of toddling. Their stance and gait will be wide legged and look more clumsy than graceful. This is why they are called toddlers. Their walk will resemble a stumbling drunk, and their speech will make the same amount of sense. The fact that they are encumbered by a nappy contributes to this unusual style, particularly if it is full. New walkers who are just getting used to balancing on two feet will be a little unstable and wobbly. However MNHI designs babies legs to become more muscular in time and as this happens their walk will become stable and sure-footed.

18 to 24 Months By the second half of their second year, even the latest of walkers will have caught up with the early developers and have graduated to climbing up and down stairs like Sir Edmund Hillary, or outlasting the competition like Steven Bradbury. The common progress is out of their highchair, onto the dining table and into the bin. MNHI warns that there is virtually nothing a toddler won't attempt to climb, as the fear and commonsense portion of the brain is still under-developed.

After climbing comes running, and for the first time as an owner you will be dealing with a fully mobile, and surprisingly fast, toddler. The days when you could sit your child down and trust that he would stay there are now officially over. Full parental attention is required

from this point on! And remember, your toddler is out of warranty so any accidental injuries caused through parental inattention could be costly.

Once your toddler learns to run he has only two settings: 'on' and 'off'. The 'on' setting is a full-on, no-holds-barred fast track to misery for the average parent, while the 'off' setting can only be described as an oasis of calm before the next storm – a calm that occurs all to infrequently, and should be accompanied by a glass of wine wherever possible.

Now your toddler is walking and running he will want to find alternative methods for getting around and keeping you on your toes, and MNHI encourages this for your child's development, if not your sanity. It's as if now that your toddler has mastered walking alone, he needs to move faster and more efficiently from calamity to calamity. For this reason MNHI suggests that a tricycle makes the ideal second birthday gift. It will give your toddler a sense of freedom while still being balanced and somewhat safe. Having said that,

ALL MNHI service centres' accessory departments have a full range of tricycles for both boy and girl toddlers as well as a comprehensive selection of protective equipment. MNHI recommends confining tricycle usage to the outdoors. The combination of a not yet fully coordinated toddler, flashing pedals and hard rubber wheels spell disaster for paint finishes and furniture alike.

MNHI warns that accidents will occur, and you should be prepared. You should never let your toddler ride a tricycle, scooter or motorised car without adequate head protection in the form of a helmet. The more over-protective owners may also opt for the added protection of knee and elbow guards, although not using this protection will not void any warranty coverage you may have in the event of scrapes and bruises. Another consequence of your toddler's new-found mobility will be his desire to stamp his independence by not wanting to travel in the pram or stroller any more, or at least only when it suits him. Up until he could walk your toddler's only way of getting around was to be strapped into a pram and pushed everywhere, but all that changes when he becomes mobile; now all he will want to do is walk and run everywhere.

That is not to say you should put the stroller in storage as toddlers get tired very quickly and very noisily, as their endurance mode is not yet fully developed, and that fierce independence can quickly turn into a barrage of whining about sore legs and tired feet. MNHI can advise owners that this tiredness will hit toddlers when least convenient for the owner and, as such, MNHI recommends that a stroller accompany any excursion outside the house (particularly to a shopping centre, the natural environment of the complaining child), until the toddler is at least four years of age.

Toddler-proofing Your Home

A toddler on the go is an accident waiting to happen. To a mobile toddler your home is a new playground full of things to touch, climb on, pull down, eat and destroy. It needn't be the nightmare it seems, and MNHI is happy to offer the following recommendations on toddler-proofing your home.

An active toddler is a time bomb waiting to go off – at any moment it could break something or hurt itself. As a responsible owner, you can prevent these accidents from occurring. In fact MNHI has found that most accidents, and accidental injuries, are entirely preventable. With a little thought, a few MNHI-approved toddler-proofing gadgets around the house, some common sense and a lot of vigilance you can significantly reduce the risk of expensive out of warranty repairs or servicing on your toddler due to misadventure. If you do not adequately toddler-proof your home, your life will become one of constant worry, work and misery, with you on the never-ending parental treadmill of following your toddler around in anticipation of intercepting the inevitable disaster. Once you have a toddler, your home becomes a place of constant tension with you trying to anticipate every move that your tiny self-destructive wrecking ball will make.

How high is high enough? When putting things out of reach of an increasingly inquisitive toddler, the answer to this question is 'too high is never high enough'. (Climbing is one of the first instincts to become activated in toddlers.) Any household cleaners that are kept under the sink must now be locked in high cupboards to prevent access to those prying toddler hands and eager toddler mouths. This is especially important as many of the common household cleaners have cartoon characters on their packaging, which make them extremely attractive to toddler eyes. What two year old wouldn't be attracted to the smiling faces of Mr Sheen and Mr Muscle, and want to put them in their mouth? Should the worst-case scenario occur and your toddler does gain access to any poisonous cleaning products, please do not hesitate to call the MNHI Poisons Advice Line.

The big things Apart from the myriad small things that need to be toddler-proofed, some of which will be covered later in this manual, it is the big things that are most likely to lead to accidents with your toddler. Sometimes the only way to keep your toddler away from harm is to make it totally inaccessible; this does not mean locking your toddler in his room, as attractive an option though this might be. This is where safety gates come in. They can be used to keep a toddler either in or out of a room and also prevent him from climbing stairs.

Toddlers are master Houdinis and doors present an exciting new world of possibilities. MNHI recommends that you keep all exterior doors, sliding doors

and screen doors locked at all times. As a closed glass sliding door can look like an open glass sliding door to an adventurous toddler, it is recommended that some form of sticker or decal be placed at eye-level to prevent your toddler walking into, or at worst, through a closed glass door. This also prevents an

Not only are MNHI-approved safety gates ideal for corralling babies, they can also be used in the containment of small dogs and puppies; preferably not at the same time as they are being used with toddlers. Also avoid using a hand-me-down gate, as not only may they be unsafe, but they could also have been subjected to substantial canine use and abuse.

owner who has had a little too much to drink from doing the same thing. Also there are rooms within the house that are high hazard, and high interest, for a toddler. (Toddlers have a built-in radar that attracts them to hazards.) MNHI recommends that these rooms should be sealed off at all times. Rooms such as the laundry with its chemicals and washing powders, and the bathroom with the combination of water and electrical appliances such as hairdryers, are best kept locked. The kitchen is another area of potential disaster – an accidental frying pan to the face can be the source of considerable pain and misery.

The little things Every parent should be aware of the big things in toddler-proofing their home, like using safety gates and keeping doors locked, but what of

Never place furniture near an open window. This will only be seen as a challenge to your average toddler. Given half a chance he will be out of the window and down the street, possibly behind the wheel of your car, before you realise it. MNHI programs its toddlers to be adventurous, and it is the owners' responsibility to be eternally vigilant.

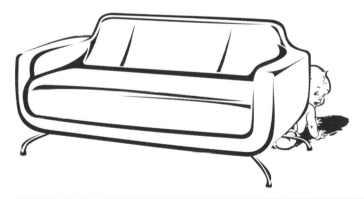

the smaller things, those everyday items that can be a source of considerable danger to the curious toddler? What follows is the MNHI guide to keeping your toddler safe from some of the less obvious hazards around the house.

Always place heavy knick-knacks or vases where your toddler can't reach them or pull them over onto himself. The same goes for potted plants, where the danger is not only from a falling pot but also from ingested dirt or potting mix. Remember to always overestimate the strength of your toddler. MNHI toddlers are equipped with an amazing will and determination when it comes to dislodging heavy items within their grasp. Their heads also seem to be a magnet for falling heavy items.

The garbage bin holds an incredible attraction to your average toddler; they see its contents, like everything else, as a source of something to put in their mouth. MNHI recommends that all garbage and recycling bins have firm fitting or lockable lids. They say that one man's trash is another man's treasure, but in the case of toddlers one man's trash is a toddler's three-course meal.

Don't place a lamp where a toddler could come in contact with a hot light bulb, and especially don't leave a lamp or other light fitting without a bulb within your toddler's reach. If there is one thing that toddlers like more than putting things in their mouth, it's sticking their fingers in them. This type of inquisitiveness is part of the MNHI inbuilt toddler exploration feature.

Placemats make the best alternative to tablecloths when you have a toddler in the house. There is nothing that a stumbling toddler likes more than to reach out and grab onto something for stability – it's part of their inbuilt stabilisation program – and in the case of a tablecloth and a table full of cutlery and crockery, this can be disastrous.

While MNHI strongly recommends that none of its babies or toddlers be exposed to cigarette smoking, it is aware that some less responsible owners will still partake in this socially unacceptable habit within the

home. It is imperative that any ashtrays be kept out of the reach of toddlers. To a toddler a handful of cigarette butts is as attractive as a steak dinner is to an adult, and

Following is a list of things that should be kept out of a toddler's reach. While MNHI cannot be held responsible for the actions of owners, we feel it responsible to publish this at times obvious list as a point of indemnity.

Sharp implements such as knives, scissors, needles, pins and razor blades should be placed well out of harm's way, as should wire coathangers. Like bowerbirds, in the mind of a toddler sharp and shiny equals something to be grabbed.

he will try to ingest them at every opportunity. Also any evidence of passive smoke damage or ingestion of cigarette butts in your toddler will instantly nullify your MNHI extended warranty.

Put away all pens, pencils and other sharp writing implements. If you do let your toddler scribble with a pen or pencil, make sure he is seated and closely supervised. Many a toddler has been brought into a

MNHI emergency service centre with an injury caused by the less than judicious use of a writing implement.

Plastic bags and plastic wrapping are other seemingly innocuous items that can cause great drama for the inquisitive toddler and should be put straight into the garbage when their use is finished. Most toddlers view a plastic bag as a hat and will place it over their head as soon as your back is turned.

MNHI acknowledges that toddler-proofing your home may seem like a lot of work, but for the continued safe and efficient running of your child it is important that you follow the guidelines as set out above. It should be noted that if you have decided to take out the MNHI extended warranty plan for your toddler, it does not cover injuries sustained through parental neglect.

Your home is no longer yours. You have become both prisoner and warder as you try to protect your toddler from himself. Your home will be barely recognisable as it becomes a maze of gates, locked doors and of things moved to places where you can no longer find them. This will be at times both frustrating and annoying, and the worst part is, it will be like this for three years.

MNHI expects a certain degree of responsibility and common sense from its owners, but in the past toddlers have presented at service centres after having swallowed some of the following: marbles, coins, buttons, safety pins, matches, thimbles, miniature cars, whistles, LED light globes, mothballs and jewellery. All of these items should be kept well away from the busy hands and mouths of your toddler. Removal of these items from your toddler's various orifices by a trained MNHI service technician can be an expensive and uncomfortable process.

Immunisation

During the first year of ownership you will have taken your baby into a prescribed MNHI service centre to have regular immunisation shots to ensure the continued trouble and illness free ownership of your baby. This regime of visits and needles continues into the toddler years of ownership as well. It should be pointed out that although your toddler is now out of the official MNHI warranty period, vaccination against several childhood illness and diseases is still covered under the MNHI extended care and responsibility package.

Following is a list of just some of the things your toddler will need to be immunised against at your local MNHI service centre to ensure maximum performance and protection: measles, mumps and rubella, as well as influenza type B, meningococcal and chickenpox. Should you have any questions or concerns regarding the vaccination of your toddler, please do not hesitate to contact your nearest MNHI service centre where a trained technician will only be too pleased to answer all your queries. Once again, MNHI cannot emphasise how important proper immunisation of your toddler is to ensuring its satisfactory long-term performance.

Toddlers don't like needles...it's a fact of life, they hurt. The child will cry, and as a result so will the co-owner if she is allowed to be present. The co-owner should not be present at any time in the toddler's life where the toddler is likely to be exposed to pain, they just get too distressed. Their partner can lose a couple of toes in a lawnmower accident and they don't care, but see their child get a needle and they come apart at the seams. Whereas a toddler who has had a needle will calm down when given a balloon and a lollypop, the co-owner normally needs a stiff vodka.

Section B:
The Terrible Twos

Now that your child has reached two years of age and is officially a toddler, a remarkable thing happens to him: he develops a certain attitude and recalcitrance that can see your little angel turn into a little monster. All MNHI babies have an inbuilt tantrum setting that is automatically engaged in the toddler's brain any time from 18 months to two years, and can stay engaged up until four years. This setting is at its peak during the period known as the terrible twos. This is also the stage of development when owners often think about

placing their child in a basket and abandoning him at a hospital or fire station. MNHI strongly recommends against this, as by this age your toddler is capable of identifying you in a line-up. Imbibing strong liquor is a much more socially acceptable course of action.

Often a parent will bring their toddler into a MNHI service centre complaining about tantrums. It has been widely thought that this situation cannot be corrected, but by using certain techniques only recently developed this situation can be somewhat rectified. Bribery is one technique. This tantrum setting – and no, it cannot be disconnected – is all about the toddler gaining independence and control, or its lack thereof. Remember that when your toddler throws a tantrum, it is just doing what it is programmed to do.

Tantrums are a toddler hallmark. In the hands of a skilful toddler, the tantrum can take on the beauty and well-planned elegance of performance art with every detail designed and played out to extract the desired reaction from the parent who is on the receiving end. Once a tantrum starts, its duration and intensity will depend entirely upon the reaction it receives. It should be noted that while MNHI takes full responsibility for the engineering of your child to throw tantrums, it takes no responsibility for how owners respond to said tantrum. It should also be noted that tantrums are inevitable; they will happen to the best of parents, and the worst. They are a fact of toddler life, but your toddler will grow out of them.

Tantrum Triggers

Apart from sheer stubbornness, what causes a toddler to have a tantrum? A good tantrum will have you questioning how many black cats have crossed your path, how many ladders have you walked under and how many mirrors have you broken, because a good tantrum will seem like the worst luck in the world has descended upon you. While a tantrum to the untrained eye can seem to be a completely random exercise in toddler futility, there are a number of reasons why tantrums are entirely appropriate and are a normal part of your child's development. They can occur for several reasons. It is important to study these reasons and judge each tantrum on its merits, like individual dives in an Olympic diving competition.

1. ***Frustration.*** It's not easy being a toddler. The child's attempts to achieve things independently are constantly being thwarted either by the adults around him or by his own limitations. It's tough trying to do things that your lack of fine motor skills won't allow you to do. Being unable to stack

blocks, button a shirt or express yourself verbally; it's all frustrating stuff and worthy of a hissy fit. Like a drunk crossing the road, a toddler knows what he wants to do but just can't manage to do it.

2. *The need to communicate.* Most toddlers are yet to have acquired the language skills to communicate with any effect, unless of course you count *Mama*, *Dadda* and *poo poo*. Let's face it, that's hardly enough to let a grown-up know that he wants the channel on the TV changed. A tantrum truly speaks louder than the few words a toddler has in his vocabulary. MNHI research and development department is looking at producing a model that develops speech earlier in life to help prevent this tantrum-inducing fault.

3. *Toddlers want to be independent* and establish their autonomy. MNHI has programmed toddlers to attempt to be their own people and to do things for themselves. They want to wobble, if not stand, on their own two feet, and when they can't do this the default tantrum setting kicks in. This sense of independence and autonomy will last through childhood and adolescence (where it will take on the form of rebellion), right up until early adulthood, when you actually want them to be independent and leave home. This is when they suddenly don't want to be so independent and decide that living at home is their best option.

4. *Wanting what they can't have.* A toddler's natural instinct is to want everything. It's the built-in

survival program. The more unattainable it is the more they want it; somewhat like a stalker. It may be a bright toy in the supermarket or a plate of ice cream, if a toddler wants it and can't have it there *will* be tears.

5. ***A lack of control over their lives.*** Toddlers live in a world of being told what they can and cannot do by their parents, so a tantrum is often the only way a toddler can express his frustration at this situation. Husbands unfortunately don't have the tantrum option to cope with this situation.

6. ***Emotions are out of control.*** All MNHI babies have an emotional core that doesn't fully develop until much later in life, which means a toddler's emotions will be all over the place and result in a tantrum. Whether happy, sad or angry, any emotional overload can cause a meltdown. This reason for throwing a tantrum will soon subside, but unfortunately it may resurface later in life as your child goes through puberty.

7. ***Hunger, overstimulation, boredom and exhaustion.*** Any one or all of these can trigger a tantrum in your toddler. In other words, a tantrum can strike at any moment and for seemingly any reason. Get ready for them, because they will happen, and happen frequently.

All MNHI toddlers are programmed to throw tantrums; only the reason, severity and duration will vary from model to model. What does a tantrum consist of? There are several stages. Initially the toddler will check to see that the intended 'victims' of the tantrum are all present. (After all, there is no use chucking a wobbly if there's no one around to watch.) The tantrum may start slowly with a bit of a high-pitched whine and a squinting of the face. Before long this whine will develop into a full-scale howl with arms beginning to flail wildly. At this point MNHI warns that all attempts to calm the toddler are fruitless and the child will often hurl himself to the ground with legs kicking out of control. At this full-blown stage, all a

parent can do is ride out the storm. As mentioned earlier, the strength and intensity of a tantrum often depends entirely upon the reaction it is getting; in technical terms, this is called the Tantrum Index.

Remain calm during a tantrum, getting into a screaming match with your toddler will only intensify his efforts, and your toddler can and will stay at it much longer than you. The longest recorded tantrum in history took place in Michigan, USA, in 1984 when three-year-old Gordon Carter threw himself on the floor on 4 December and the screaming didn't stop until 6 December. The reason? He didn't want to wear gloves and a hat to go outside. Remember, tantrums are normal; your toddler is not broken and does not need to be taken to a MNHI service centre for repair.

Warning No. 1 MNHI cautions that in its most intense form, a tantrum may result in breath-holding. Breath-holding starts out as a regular tantrum, but the crying and screaming intensifies. Soon your toddler will be turning red in the face with unbridled fury. Then, without notice, the screaming stops – not because the tantrum is over but because your toddler has started holding his breath! The lips begin to turn blue due to a lack of oxygen, eventually the skin will turn blue and if the breath is held long enough the toddler may pass out. While this may be disturbing for the owner, rest assured it is perfectly safe for the toddler, and you will probably enjoy the few short moments of peace and quiet. The loss of consciousness is actually a MNHI pre-programmed protective response

that allows normal breathing to resume without any harm being done to the toddler. Owners should be careful of the one major downside to breath-holding. The act itself is so confronting that you may become more likely to give in to the toddler just to avoid the circumstances that might lead to it. Toddlers are programmed to sense weakness, in the same way that wild animals can sense fear, and it won't be long before your toddler reaches the conclusion that 'by holding my breath I get my own way'. MNHI recommends that you treat breath-holding in the same way you would treat any other tantrum. Should the toddler pass out, give him a cuddle when he comes around but under no circumstances give in to what it was he tantrummed about in the first place.

Warning No. 2 Another extreme form of tantrum is head-banging. Some toddlers, when in a full-blown tantrum, will throw themselves on the ground and start banging their head. Although this looks extreme, they rarely hurt themselves. MNHI has designed the toddler cranium to be extremely resilient to this form of behaviour. Head-banging tantrums are usually short-lived as the toddler soon learns that self-inflicted pain is a poor way of making a point. Head-banging should be approached as if it were any other tantrum: simply act unimpressed and ignore it while trying to divert the toddler's attention elsewhere. If it continues, let the tantrum play itself out. Toddlers may lack sense but they are not stupid, and they will soon tire of the display. Another way to cure your toddler of head-banging is to film one of his displays and post the results on YouTube. Even at the tender age of two or three a toddler will understand the theory of public humiliation.

Owner Behaviour During a Tantrum

How you as the owner react to your toddler's tantrums will determine the strength and duration of future tantrums. A tantrum can be quite confronting and more than a little embarrassing if it takes place in public. Often the best course of action to take when dealing with a tantrum is **no action at all**. A toddler who is ignored during a tantrum will get it out of his system faster. Once you have established that your toddler is safe (this is particularly relevant for toddlers who like to kick and thrash around during a tantrum), MNHI suggests you just go about your business as if nothing unusual is going on. This may be hard if your toddler is a 'thrower' who likes to launch toys and other missiles during a tantrum. Make it clear that you have no interest in the unseemly display your child is putting on, perhaps by switching on the television or doing some housework, but keep moving as you will be less of an easy target for any projectile that may be launched mid-tantrum. Soon your toddler will come to realise that it's just not worth getting all worked up when no one is paying attention, and the tantrums will be come less violent and less frequent. Do not take the next step beyond ignoring the tantrum and laugh at your toddler, as this will only serve to further enrage him. No one likes to be laughed at, especially when you are doing your best to be understood by throwing a tantrum as well as anything else you can get your hands on.

If you do decide the silent treatment isn't the best course of action, MNHI offers up the following tips for confronting a tantrum head on.

First of all, it is best to speak softly. It is important to remember that all MNHI toddlers are equipped with the best lungs on the market today and trying to scream over all that screaming will only be seen as a challenge to an already irate toddler. A quiet, even tone of voice will tell the toddler that you are in control (even though you probably aren't), and should help the toddler calm down, though maybe not straight away.

Try expressing empathy with the toddler. This will either calm or further enrage him. Telling your toddler that you know it's hard when he can't get

what he wants can backfire if he has a sense of what the word 'condescending' means.

Try holding the toddler. Trying to hold your toddler mid-tantrum might seem like walking into the eye of a cyclone, but it just might work. A tight hold (as opposed to the strangling squeeze you actually want to give him) during a tantrum can have the effect of dissolving anger in both toddler and parent. At best, the hold will dissolve into a hug and all is calm. At worst, the hug will be viewed by the toddler as an act of aggression and the tantrum will intensify. If all else fails, MNHI suggests that the responsible owner ceases the hug and reverts back to simply ignoring the tantrum.

MNHI hosts tantrum information evenings on the first Tuesday of every month at all of its service centres. These evenings may be of interest if you are having particular problems when it comes to controlling or coping with your toddler's tantrums.

The public tantrum. It doesn't take too long for a toddler to realise that the most effective place to throw a tantrum is in a crowded public place. Whether it be the supermarket or a packed shopping centre, when a public tantrum happens it will trigger certain responses in the owner. The first is acute embarrassment. The instinctive reaction to this behaviour is to deny all responsibility and pretend that the child is someone else's. This only works until the word *Dad* is thrown up as part of the tantrum. Ignoring the child, as you would at home, becomes impractical in the public setting, especially when no matter what you do at least half of the horrified onlookers will think that you got it wrong and consider you a second-rate parent. In which case, MNHI suggests that you just give in and let the toddler have what he wants. Although that advice flies in the face of all the other advice given in this section, it is also important to remember that picking your battles is an equally important part of being a responsible owner.

The Do's and Don'ts

Just as important as the things that the owner of a toddler must do during a tantrum are the things that an owner must avoid. It is crucial that as an owner you do not have a tantrum of your own, particularly in public, as this will only serve to attract all sorts of unwanted advice from those around you who think they know better; particularly the elderly. MNHI strongly suggests that you remain in complete control of the situation at all times. It is a fact that all MNHI toddlers are engineered to throw tantrums just as they are engineered to sense fear and a loss of control in a parent and to capitalise on that situation.

Do not punish a tantrum. As stated previously, all MNHI toddlers are programmed to tantrum so there is little point in punishment, either during or after a tantrum. The best course of action for the father is to try to ride out the tantrum and to let the malfunctioning toddler self-correct its behaviour. Although not strictly recommended, in extreme cases bribery can be useful.

Under no circumstances should you try to reason or argue with an out of control toddler; he is simply beyond reason. Trying to gain the upper hand with a toddler mid-tantrum is as futile as trying to catch lightning in a bottle; and more dangerous. All logic is lost on a toddler having a meltdown. Telling him that he doesn't need that Kinder Surprise because there is chocolate at home will get you nowhere.

When the tantrum is over, and every tantrum ends despite how it feels at the time, try to let it go. Don't revisit the episode or lecture the child about what has just happened, and especially don't demand an apology or an admission of guilt, because in the toddler's eyes he didn't actually do anything wrong. He is just acting in the way that MNHI programmed him to act. Demanding an apology from a toddler is just as likely to bring on another tantrum. Toddlers are a lot like politicians in this regard.

If it was your refusal to give in to a demand that set your toddler off in the first place, don't give in now that the situation has calmed down. This will only give your toddler the impression that tantrums work.

One point that MNHI stresses in regards to tantrums is isolation. Should your toddler throw a tantrum, it is vital that you separate him from any other toddlers in the vicinity. Although all MNHI toddlers are engineered for independence, a tantrum is contagious. If one toddler goes off, it will trigger a chain reaction in all toddlers within earshot (just like barking dogs). Should such a chain reaction occur, do not panic. It is not a fault in your child; it is merely the inbuilt protection mode kicking in. This protection mode is designed for the safety of the group. If one toddler registers peril or discomfort, the other will join in to gain the attention of an owner who will hopefully remedy the situation.

Tantrums are the most common and least desirable trait of the terrible twos and are to be expected. Should your toddler have temper tantrums more than twice a day, however, and should they be excessively violent or aggressive and you have trouble correcting them then MNHI suggests that perhaps your toddler may need some extra help from a qualified MNHI behavioural technician. An appointment can be made at your nearest MNHI service centre.

Section C:
Eating, Sleeping and Toilet Training

In this section of the manual we shall deal with the advanced fuelling and waste disposal systems that your toddler has developed or is in the process of developing. A lot has changed in your baby, and soon that once bottle-fed angel will become a self-feeding mess-creating machine. And to top it all off, nappies will soon be a thing of the past and your toddler will need to be taught the ways of the toilet.

MNHI has carefully engineered the internal workings of your toddler to grow and adapt to its changing fuel requirements. In other words, what goes in must come out, and as what goes in changes, what comes out also must change. Colour and consistency are the two key-words for both functions and as one changes so must the other. Through following this section, by the time your toddler reaches 36 months he will be using cutlery and the toilet like a seasoned professional.

Giving Up the Bottle

One of the key steps in introducing your toddler to a new solid food source is to wean him off the bottle and onto the cup. Weaning is the process that MNHI has designed your toddler to go through to transition between liquid and solid fuel. The bottle has been your baby's source of nutrition virtually since day one (apart from the co-owner's role in breastfeeding – a role in which the owner plays no part apart other than to provide a sympathetic ear) and your toddler is now ready to say goodbye to formula and bottles and hello to cow's milk, sippy cups and solids.

MNHI recommends that weaning take place from 12 months, or at the end of the warranty period, so that the process is complete by the time your toddler reaches the terrible twos, at which point the owner will have plenty of other issues to contend with. There will be enough tantrums to deal with at this stage without having the added stress and anxiety created by bottle withdrawal.

When it's time to say bye-bye to the bottle, MNHI recommends a quick withdrawal; especially if your toddler is relatively easy going, doesn't react adversely to change, isn't particularly hooked on the bottle and has already shown interest in the cup. If all of these descriptors fit your toddler then cold turkey weaning is for you.

Weaning should be like removing a bandaid and done in one quick, clean movement. Set aside a day for the commencement of cold turkey weaning and try to keep it clear of any other distractions. When it comes time for the mid-morning refuel, simply replace the bottle with a sippy cup. MNHI suggests that you talk up the enormity of the situation and point out that your toddler is now a big boy or girl and can drink from a cup just like Mummy and Daddy. Make no mistake, this is a big occasion for your toddler and the bigger the fuss you make, the more smoothly the transition from bottle to cup is likely to go.

If your toddler is into new possessions, and what toddler isn't, mark the special day with a trip to the MNHI sales and service centre to purchase a brand-new big kid cup. (Reverse psychology is a vital tool in the parent's arsenal when it comes to instigating any change in a toddler's life.) Once you have let your toddler select a new 'big kid cup', why not have a ceremony to say goodbye to the bottle? All MNHI service centres have a bottle recycling bin for just such an occasion, so that when you are picking up a new sippy cup your toddler can say goodbye to the bottle by throwing it in the bin; it adds a certain finality to the changeover that is both cathartic and environmentally friendly. (Note: All bottles recycled through the MNHI service centres are completely cleaned and sterilised then distributed to third world countries.) Although not strictly recommended, MNHI knows of several owners who have purchased sippy cups for themselves with the express purpose of drinking alcohol in the car, reasoning that no police officer would be suspicious of a sippy cup.

It is important to remember that the bottle is for fuelling your toddler and providing sucking comfort. The point of a sippy cup is to deliver fluids to your toddler's operating system. The sippy cup should not be used to calm down a stressed toddler, or to prevent boredom from setting in when on an outing, or to keep little hands and mouths occupied. (Although it must be pointed out that at times of stress for both father and toddler, the giving of a sippy cup can provide welcome relief for both.)

One of the keys to successful weaning is for the owner to stay patient, which can be easier said than done. Depending upon how attached your toddler is to the bottle, you can expect some tough times on weaning day and possibly the days ahead. Some say it is easier to get off cigarettes than it is to get off the bottle, and your toddler may suffer withdrawals. Should you find the weaning process a difficult and challenging one,

MNHI is happy to offer a reasonably priced in-house weaning service at all of its service centres. Simply make an appointment and drop your toddler into the service centre by 8.30am with his bottle and sippy cup and our trained technicians will have your little one weaned and ready to go for a lunchtime pick-up. MNHI forbids owners to stay for the duration of the intensive weaning service as it may cause distress.

Brushing Teeth

MNHI has designed your toddler so that by the time he reaches 24 to 30 months he will have a full set of 20 teeth. These teeth have been engineered to last between five to ten years and will take your toddler through all the rudimentary stages of the ingestion of solid fuel and beyond. By following the guidelines as set out here you, and eventually your toddler, should be able to care and maintain these teeth without difficulty. It is important that you commence regular

brushing once your toddler starts growing teeth. This brushing should take place at least twice a day; after breakfast and before bedtime.

Brushing your toddler's teeth should be fun. If you make it seem like a chore, the less inclined he will be to let you do it. Not all toddlers take to having their teeth brushed and often fear can be a good motivator to encourage them. This is where an elderly relative with dentures can come in handy. Nothing frightens a toddler into wanting good oral hygiene more than having an old person pull out their false teeth in front of them. Some boy toddlers may actually think that this is a cool trick but, for the most part, children find the sight horrifying.

When selecting a toothbrush for your toddler, choose one with soft bristles and a small head. MNHI service centres stock a range of approved toothbrushes that are decorated with bright colours and lights that flash to help make brushing more appealing. Remember that for the entire toddler period of your child's life, you will be in charge of brushing his teeth, with him often not being able to effectively brush until the age of five or six. This is a deliberate MNHI design feature, meant to keep owners involved in the vital function of dental hygiene for as long as possible.

Brush your toddler's teeth as you would your own, working over each tooth in a circular motion and remembering to rinse thoroughly when the job is done. Further information regarding dental hygiene and flossing your toddler's teeth is available in the supplementary handbook.

Some toddlers will stubbornly refuse to have their teeth brushed; like so many other aspects of their life it is all part of them trying to stamp their autonomy. Unlike other battles where it is just as easy to give in to as to fight, MNHI suggests that this one is non-negotiable and a responsible owner must insist on tooth-brushing without compromise. Like most behavioural changes, one method recommended by MNHI to help your child get used to brushing his teeth is to let him have a go at it unaided, at least at first. This will allow your toddler to get used to the feel of brushing before you take over and do the job properly.

Toddler teeth come with an extended six-year warranty against corrosion and cavities. However, if upon inspection it is revealed that inadequate care has been taken in the maintenance of these teeth, this warranty will be automatically become void.

Feeding

Prior to weaning and before your toddler begins to eat properly he will need to gradually be introduced to solid food (in this case 'solid' means pureed). This process should have already taken place at approximately six months of age and any problems encountered with this process would be covered under your child's 12 month all-inclusive warranty. It should be noted that all equipment (spoons, bowls etc.) for this transition can be purchased from your nearest MNHI service centre as can a range of suitable 'starter foods' all designed to meet your child's growing refuelling demands.

Self-feeding is the next step in your toddler's development. Once your toddler begins to grab and reach for the spoon you are feeding him with, the time is right to commence an attempt at self-feeding. MNHI warns that the road to self-feeding can be a frustrating one for the toddler's owner. At times it will seem there is more food on the toddler, the floor and even on you than actually gets eaten. Stick with it though, as eventually the fine motor skills that are required for self-feeding, and which are installed in all MNHI babies at the time of delivery, will come good and everything will fall into place. Initial self-feeding should be approached by the owner as if he were painting a room of the house; there will be mess, so old clothes and plenty of drop sheets are recommended.

Here's what MNHI has programmed your toddler to do, and what you can expect on the road to self-feeding:

12 to 15 Months A MNHI toddler at 12 months should be highly skilled in picking up food and shovelling it into his mouth. If your toddler has a liking for these 'finger foods' then keep serving them up to him; eating food this way will help increase the hand–eye coordination so vital in later cutlery use. Shortly after his first birthday your toddler will start to show interest in using a spoon, though not necessarily for eating. The technique will be clumsy and messy at first as interest outweighs skill, but it is vital practice and MNHI recommends encouraging this behaviour to ensure a smooth transition to the inevitable self-feeding of solid fuel.

15 to 18 Months By this stage most toddlers have made the mental connection between spoon, fork and bowl and how they all work together to end up with food in the mouth. But when it comes to being able to combine all three is an entirely different story. Although MNHI programs its toddlers to be able to do this, mastering the technique takes longer in some toddlers than others. First the food must be scooped into the spoon, then the spoon must be lifted to the mouth, all without tipping the spoon up and dumping its contents all over the floor, then the food must be delicately manoeuvred into the mouth for consumption. And that is just the first mouthful, there is a whole meal to go! This is a very messy job, and at times a very frustrating job for the owner, but to get the self-feeding process for the solid fuel perfect it must be practiced over and over, like a good golf shot.

18 to 24 Months By the time your toddler reaches 18 months it will be very difficult to extract the spoon from his hand. Toddlers are engineered to do things themselves and will verbalise their willingness to do so. Owners should not expect neat eating yet – there

> Never overfeed your toddler. Like adults, toddlers will only eat when they are hungry. By overfeeding your toddler you can upset its delicate fuel in–fuel out balance and cause problems with the internal workings of the body. If your toddler is not hungry he simply won't eat, just as when he is hungry he will demand food. MNHI has designed its babies this way to maintain the appropriate refuelling and waste disposal equilibrium.

will still be a large amount of spillage – but you can expect your toddler to start understanding the rules; that is, if you throw your vegetables off the plate, lunch will be over. Starvation is a powerful, though not recommended, motivator. At this stage your toddler should be ready for a regular cup when it comes to liquid fuelling. At the very least he should be drinking comfortably with a straw. If your toddler isn't self-feeding finger foods by 18 months, it is important that you take him to a MNHI service centre for assessment. Our trained technicians will be able to help resolve those issues.

Sleeping

As your toddler becomes more active, MNHI has designed him to need a decreased amount of sleep, and his daytme sleeps will occur at different times from when he was a baby. The one downside to this is that as your toddler becomes more active the less sleep he will want to have. As the total number of sleep hours decreases, your toddler's sleep cycles will

become more mature and more adult-like, even if his behaviour doesn't. MNHI has designed children at the toddler stage to have one or two naps during the day and to sleep all the way through the night. But be warned, toddlers do not like sleep: they are in the stage of activity and exploration where time spent in bed is seen as time wasted.

> **Warning** A tired toddler is as much a handful as a hungry toddler. The risk of tantrums increases exponentially should he miss a sleep or not get enough sleep. For every sleep a toddler misses, it is proven that each resulting tantrum can take up to 12 minutes of the owner's expected lifespan!

MNHI makes the following sleep recommendations for the satisfactory operation of your toddler. These are recommendations only, as sleep times will vary according to activity levels and parental manufactured environment. A 12-month-old child needs about 14 hours of sleep in each 24-hour period, 11 hours of which should be at night with the remainder spread across two daytime sleeps. At 18 months your toddler should be still sleeping 11 hours at night, with a slight reduction in daytime sleep to around two hours. At 24 months the pattern is similar, with 11 hours of sleep at night and one afternoon nap of between one and two hours.

By not allowing their child to get the recommended amount of sleep owners are acting in direct contradiction to MNHI specifications and, as such, will void any extended warranty or service plans the owner may have taken out. MNHI acknowledges that all toddlers will have differing sleep patterns, and the figures provided in this manual are a rough guide as to what can be expected. In reality, toddler sleep is an entirely random affair and may involve bed-wetting and nightmares.

Few toddlers look forward to bedtime. This is the period of their lives where they have been engineered for activity. Therefore, the prospect of enforced down-time does not sit well with them, and they will resist with all their strength. The other thing that toddlers are engineered to do is to question their parents: just because Daddy says I should do something in not a good enough reason for me to do it. And this instinct is particularly prevalent at sleep time.

As toddler sleep matures they begin to dream more. This is the pre-programmed imagination part of the brain. As this part of the brain develops the dreams can become more intense. A scary dream, or nightmare, can wake a toddler and keep him from settling back down for fear of being alone. Under no circumstances does MNHI suggest allowing your toddler into your bed after a nightmare. Doing this will set a dangerous and hard to break precedent that will ultimately affect your sleep and lovemaking. These new fears in your toddler's life may also manifest themselves as a fear of the dark. If this is the case, MNHI suggests a night-light for your toddler. A night-light should cast a friendly glow in the room and not be so bright that it casts potentially disturbing shadows. Should waking after a scary dream become too frequent, it is important to book your toddler into a MNHI service centre for a thorough check-up and comprehensive sleep analysis.

To make like easier for you and your toddler, MNHI makes the following suggestions in aiding you to establish good sleep patterns in your toddler:

1. *Set up a regular bedtime routine.* The right evening ritual performed night after night will help your toddler unwind and also assist in bridging the gap between awake time and sleep time. This routine is crucial and may include reading

books, talking about what you did during your day or simply singing songs. Be flexible when trying to find the right bedtime for your toddler. MNHI doesn't engineer its toddlers to sleep at a certain time. That time can only be found by trial and error. Some toddlers find it more difficult to unwind than others and a later sleep time is appropriate.

2. *Do not let your toddler sleep in.* Waking up at the same time each day is just as important in establishing a good sleep pattern as going to sleep at the same time. One little sleep-in (regardless of how enjoyable it is for the owner) can throw out your toddler's sleep cycles for a day or two with disastrous results.

3. Importantly, it is vital that you *maintain total control over the sleep time ritual.* Never yell, threaten or make deals. The more unfazed you are in the war zone that can sometimes be bedtime, the more your toddler realises that you mean business.

Should, despite following this advice, you still be experiencing difficulties when it comes to putting your toddler to sleep, MNHI conducts sleep schools at each of its service centres on the first Wednesday of each month. Simply bring your toddler and any toys he may sleep with to the service centre and one of our trained technicians will take you through the basics of toddler sleep patterns. Please note that the cost of these classes is non-refundable should your toddler react adversely to the techniques demonstrated on the day.

Toilet Training

When is the right time for toddlers to change from the portable waste disposal units (nappies) and start using the potty? MNHI suggests that there is no specific time at which this change can take place.

What sort of potty should I buy? MNHI manufactures a number of approved potty training aids, all of which are available from the accessories department of all service centres. The best sort of potty is one that is durable and stable so it won't tip over when your toddler jumps up to check his progress. Also available is a potty seat that attaches to the adult toilet seat. This is recommended as a second stage seat once your toddler has mastered the smaller ground level potty. MNHI does not recommend the use of novelty potties, particularly one popular model shaped like a turtle. This puts an unrealistic expectation in the toddler's mind about what turtles are used for and can lead to embarrassment when visiting the zoo.

All MNHI toddlers are designed to pick up basic toilet skills at their own speed, and when this happens has no relation to other areas of development, such as walking. Most MNHI toddlers master the art of toilet use between 24 and 36 months. Interestingly, girl toddlers master the toilet on average four months sooner than boy model toddlers. MNHI has designed this feature deliberately to compensate for the extra time boy models will spend on the toilet in later years.

When it comes to toilet training, all MNHI toddlers are quite simply ready when they are ready. Although MNHI engineers all its toddlers to exacting specifications, it is important to let the toddler set the pace. If you try to force the situation, all the best plans and tactics in the world will fail. There are certain inbuilt signs you should watch out for which indicate your toddler is ready to commence toilet training. If you find you are changing fewer wet nappies, this is a welcome sign. Until about 20 months toddlers go through the liquid waste disposal procedure so often that expecting them to be able to control themselves

MNHI recommends the use of correct terminology for your toddler's bodily functions. Whatever terms you use, they will be the ones your toddler picks up and there is nothing more embarrassing than being in public with your toddler and he declares that he needs a 'dump'.

is unrealistic. But if your toddler has begun staying dry for an hour or two, and even sometimes wakes dry then he may be ready to begin the toilet training procedure.

Another pre-programmed sign that your toddler is ready to commence toilet training is when he begins to verbalise the fact that he is disposing of waste. Once he is aware that he is voiding and he lets you know, this is a sure sign of toilet readiness.

To be ready to undergo toilet training, your toddler must be able to undress himself. When the time comes, the potty won't be of much use unless your toddler can quickly pull down his pants in preparation. Accidents at this stage can adversely affect the

Now that your toddler is taking in more solid fuel during his second year he will probably create less solid waste. Expect an average of between 4 and 20 solid waste disposal actions per week, depending on fuel and fluid intake and individual internal workings. When it comes to a healthy solid waste disposal, consistency is more important than frequency. As long as the solid waste is soft and easy to pass, then your toddler's operating systems are functioning to specification. Small, hard and difficult to pass solid waste may signal constipation, just as watery, frequent and loose solid waste may be diarrhoea. MNHI suggests the owner makes an appointment to see a technician for advice on how to correct these problems.

As part of the MNHI Platinum Extended Warranty package we offer a very exclusive one-on-one demonstration option. MNHI has found that toddlers learn by example, and we also understand that not all owners are comfortable doing their business with an audience. As a result, MNHI has assembled a highly specialised team of technicians to help with this problem. Just bring your toddler into the service centre where he will be taken into a hygienic custom-made individual toilet cubicle and our qualified technician will demonstrate how to squat, push, wipe and flush. It is important to note when making your booking for this service that you specify the gender of your toddler so that we can organise a technician with the same 'equipment' as your child.

mindset of your toddler and severely set back the whole toilet training process.

When your toddler starts talking the talk, he is ready to start walking the walk. Whatever terminology you choose to use for the process of waste disposal with your toddler, whether slang or technical, once he is aware of the terms and what they mean and can use them at the correct time, MNHI recommends that he is ready to start toilet training.

Some MNHI toddlers have an inbuilt fear of the toilet. Some believe that if they sit on the toilet they will fall in and drown. Others are terrified by the sound a flushing toilet makes. In both cases, try starting out with a potty. They can sit comfortably on the pot without the fear of falling in and there is no flush to scare them.

As with the transition from liquid to solid fuel, the transition to self-waste disposal is not an exact science. It may take several attempts to get your toddler going to the toilet in the manner you would like. This transition will be as equally messy as the road to self-feeding, only more pungent. Remember, MNHI programs its toddlers to develop at slightly different rates depending upon which model you have and the domestic circumstances of the owner.

The day your toddler stops wearing nappies is a day to celebrate. As an owner you are no longer slave to the nappy, the nappy bag, the wipes, the talc and every other thing associated with changing nappies both at home and away; and that's even before you consider saying goodbye to the smell and mess. So, why not have a little celebration? Gather yourself, the co-owner and your newly toilet-independent toddler in the backyard and have a ceremonial burning of the nappy. You will find it a fitting goodbye to something that has brought you so much misery. Just one quick point, MNHI strongly suggests the burning of a new nappy and not a used one.

Getting Dressed

Around the time that your toddler is mastering the art of going to the toilet, he will be wanting to dress himself in 'big kids' clothes'. This can be a frustrating time for toddlers as they attempt to master the

intricacies of buttons and zips, with their chubby little fingers and fine motor skills not yet fully developed. MNHI has designed these frustrations to be part of the toddler development software installed in all of its babies.

Your toddler will show interest in dressing himself from about 12 months, although he won't fully perfect it until closer to 36 months. To make this transition easier MNHI suggests that you look for easy to pull on pants, shirts and skirts with elastic waistbands and large neck openings and, where possible, avoid buttons and zips. Practice makes perfect and there will be a certain amount of self-satisfaction if toddlers are allowed to do the job themselves with minimal help, despite the fact that you may be in a hurry to leave the house. As with all toddler self-determination processes, mastering this skill will be frustrating.

Some common toddler dressing issues MNHI regularly encounters are toddlers who put both legs into one leg hole and putting shirts on backwards. These are problems that are encountered by all owners and toddlers and by no way indicate that your toddler is faulty. We reiterate: it just takes time and practice. Should you feel your toddler is making no progress with self-dressing (and this will particularly be the case with socks), owners can call the nearest MNHI service centre for advice.

Bathing

Now that your toddler is no longer a baby, bath time will take on a whole new complexion. Toddlers aren't known for being hygiene crazy and often will go to any lengths to avoid it, and this includes baths. By now your toddler has progressed from the baby bath to the adult bath, and for some this is a little daunting. To make the transition easier MNHI suggests introducing toys to the situation, as a distracted toddler is easier to pin down and clean. It's amazing what a few boats can do in terms of diverting attention from the job at hand. Of course MNHI stipulates the use of warm water only in the bath for toddlers, as any damage to the skin caused by scalding will automatically void any warranty coverage.

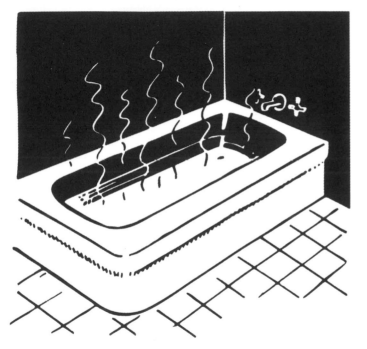

If the bathtub still triggers a negative response from your toddler, try letting him accompany you into the shower instead. It may take some time for him to adjust to the water falling from the ceiling, but once he does you will find he will gladly hop under the shower alone. It is important that when accompanying a toddler in the shower that you position him close to the wall in case he slips. If he is not near the wall and slips, he will reach out and grab anything to balance himself, and in the case of the father this can be painful.

MNHI suggests the use of a mild soap solution when washing your toddler, to wash from top to bottom, and then immediately rinse with clear water. Bath time is also the perfect time to inspect your toddler for any damage he may have incurred during the day. Toddlers pick up all manner of scrapes and grazes that you can be unaware of until you conduct a thorough examination.

Section D:
Correcting Bad Habits and Unwanted Behaviour

Although MNHI builds its toddlers to exacting standards they arc in no way perfect and, depending upon environmental circumstances and owner discipline, they will develop bad habits. These habits do not in any way indicate that your toddler is faulty or that you as an owner have done a bad job, they merely demonstrate the inventiveness of the toddler brain.

Even the nicest of toddlers can display some of the nastiest of habits, and this will be extremely frustrating for the owner.

A lot of the bad habits displayed by toddlers are learned behaviours from other toddlers. Because MNHI has designed toddlers to be excellent mimics to survive, they learn bad habits really easily. A new habit will generally find favour with a toddler for around a week or two, only to be dropped in favour of another habit that has caught his attention. Unless, of course, you as the owner seem to find the habit particularly annoying, in which case it can stay around for a good bit longer.

Biting

Biting is one of the more common bad habits displayed by MNHI toddlers and is mostly found in toddlers aged between 18 and 24 months. It's like they have just discovered their teeth and think there are better uses to put them to than just chewing food. At this age biting is not part of a premeditated plan

to hurt others but more a symptom of the age and of an under-developed sense of right and wrong. A bite is an impulse: to a toddler it just seems like a good idea at the time. MNHI has designed its toddlers with an inbuilt survival system, and part of that system is to eat once their teeth have grown through. In some toddlers this instinct extends beyond food and unfortunately may be exercised on other humans and, in extreme cases, pets.

More often than not, the biting impulse is directed towards fellow family members, be that owner, co-owner or sibling. In this scenario it is easy to remove the offending toddler from the situation and let him think about what he has done. It won't take a toddler long to realise that if he bites then he will be put in 'solitude' and the habit will soon break. Should your toddler bite a friend or neighbour, however, there is an expectation that the punishment meted should be a little more severe than a mere time-out.

MNHI believes that a time-out will suffice as punishment to biting behaviour, and under no circumstances should the responsible toddler owner over-react to this situation. Furthermore, regardless of the pressure being applied by the parent of the victim, or your neighbour or friend, the behaviour should not be treated with a smack. Smacking has not been recommended by MNHI for the treatment of unruly toddlers since 1984 and should smacking be found to take place at a routine maintenance inspection, MNHI is bound to make a full report to the relevant authorities.

It is important that you get to the biting habit quickly and nip it (so to speak) in the bud. If your child becomes known in social and neighbourhood circles as a 'biter' then it will severely impact the amount of social interaction he will be exposed to as other owners will prevent their toddlers from playing with him. Being known as a 'biter' is one of the worst things your child can be known as; just behind being known as a 'smearer'. And if you have a biting smearer on your hands then heaven help you.

Although it seems a major issue at the time it occurs, and perhaps reoccurs, MNHI is happy to advise owners that biting is only a passing phase as your toddler comes to grips with having teeth and what they are for. Biting should pass by the time your toddler comes in for his 36 months major service, and if it hasn't one of our highly trained psychological services technicians will be available to work with you and your toddler to reach a solution.

Hitting

It should be noted that MNHI suggests the same treatment for a hitter as we do a biter. The motives and reasons are nearly always the same, it is just the method of pain delivery that varies. Never hit a child who has hit another child. Apart from voiding warranties, it sends the wrong message that it is okay to hit. As with biting, should your toddler hit someone who is not within your family circle, you will feel undue pressure to punish your child more severely than you would if your toddler has hit a sibling. Resist this pressure and just stick to time out as a punishment.

Self-exploration

As your toddler grows and develops it is engineered to explore and understand its own body. Unfortunately,

sometimes this can take the form of the antisocial habit of playing with its private parts. Most toddlers will play with their genitals at one time or another;

it has no sexual overtones, they just enjoy it. MNHI is very to keen to point out several important facts to toddler owners regarding this practice. First, it will not send your toddler mad, deaf or blind. It may cause some mild embarrassment should it take place in public but MNHI is here to assure you that there will be no lasting side effects to this behaviour. Second, this is not a learned behaviour. Your toddler isn't copying something it has seen; unless, of course, your toddler has been watching the late night editions of *Big Brother*.

This habit usually begins in the second year, when the nappy region is revealed and the toddler suddenly has a whole new area of the body to explore. Self-exploration is particularly prevalent in the boy model toddler, where there is much more of interest in the area to play with. MNHI would like to point out that this area of the toddler's body is quite robust and will be able to stand up to whatever 'punishment' it will be dealt.

Many owners are quite shocked to see their toddler engaging in this behaviour and can react accordingly. MNHI advises against a negative and stern reaction. This completely innocent habit should be ignored, not corrected, and MNHI advises parents to relax and try not to burden their innocent toddler with their own hang-ups. However, should your toddler be overdoing it a bit on the fiddling front (and let's face it, it's quite difficult to concentrate on the evening news while your boy toddler is sitting in the corner having a go at himself), MNHI suggests that you try to divert his attention towards another activity.

One area where your toddler having his hands down his pants could be a little embarrassing is in public. If you should find yourself in this situation, once again try not to make a big deal out of the situation, after all your toddler is only doing something which to him is completely natural and the only one getting embarrassed is you. The key in this situation is not to humiliate or punish your toddler but instead, gently persuade him to remove the offending hand from his pants and divert his attention with something more interesting. All MNHI service centre spare parts and accessory departments have a range of toys and novelties that you can carry with you to produce as diversions at the appropriate time.

Nose-picking

As mentioned earlier in this manual toddlers love to stick their fingers in things, whether it's a light socket or a doorjamb. Unfortunately, this love of digital exploration also leads to one of the toddler's worst habits: sticking their fingers up their nose. MNHI has designed children to react to boredom and tiredness in a number of ways, and inserting a finger into a nostril is an unintended result of this boredom setting. Like all toddler bad habits, nose-picking can reflect very poorly on the owner and be the cause of severe embarrassment if it takes place in public. Of

course should your toddler decide to eat the results of his impromptu mining excursion, it becomes really embarrassing and steps must be taken.

Once again, as with other boredom-based bad habits, the best cure for nose-picking is distraction. If you can keep those little hands busy and that little mind active, there is less chance that stray fingers will find themselves heading into nostrils. Also, fear is a good motivator with a toddler when it comes to this problem. Good results can be achieved by telling the offending youngster that 'if you don't stop picking your nose, your head will cave in!' Should distraction and fear not correct this problem, MNHI has designed a mask-like cover for the nasal region that prevents fingers being inserted yet still allows breathing to take place. This device is available from the accessories department at all MNHI service centres.

Hair-pulling

Many toddlers are brought into our service centres with their owners complaining about hair-pulling. For those toddlers who have still to master a fair vocabulary, grabbing hold of the nearest head of hair and giving it a yank is a type of fallback communication, not unlike hitting and biting. Like those bad habits, hair-pulling is an antisocial behaviour often brought about by the toddler being frustrated with the environment, or his own ability or lack thereof to communicate his needs.

The best course of correction is to remove the toddler from the situation and let things calm down before reintroducing the child. Should your toddler demonstrate any or all of the big three aggressive behaviours (biting, hitting and hair-pulling), prepare yourself to be judged by everyone who witnesses the offence taking place.

When it comes to toddler discipline everyone is an expert, but just follow the MNHI guidelines and your toddler will be on the road to breaking these bad habits before you know it. You may find yourself regularly apologising to the parents of your toddler's victims, but at least you know you have the knowledge of MNHI's years of toddler experience backing you up.

The Escapologist

MNHI toddlers have been designed to two distinct specifications. At the time of ordering you cannot specify which variant you want, and a number of factors including your parenting will determine which way your toddler develops. On one hand there is the toddler that does everything he is meant to in terms of being obedient and not wanting to leave his owner's side. The other toddler is the one that is the escape artist; the one that will run off and abscond at the first opportunity, often resulting in him getting himself lost.

While running away may seem like a playful game of hide-and-seek to your toddler, the fact is there are any number of hazards that await the adventurous toddler. Stairs, escalators, lifts and traffic are all huge threats to a runner. Although MNHI acknowledges that ultimately we have supplied you with a toddler that has a tendency to abscond, we take no responsibility for any injuries done or damage caused while your toddler is out of your sight or control.

MNHI acknowledges that having a toddler that is a runner can be a trial. Owners of these will find themselves constantly on their toes, ready at a moment's notice to take part in a high-speed pursuit out of the playground or through the shopping centre. Should you be the parent of a runner, MNHI advises that when you take your child to a public place ensure he is wearing a distinctive item of clothing; perhaps an animal print shirt or brightly coloured hat. This will make identification easier when the inevitable lost child announcement is made.

If your toddler is a runner you can assume that at some stage he will get away from you. MNHI advises that upon leaving the house your toddler should have some form of identification on him at all times; perhaps even with your mobile phone number on it. MNHI can supply a wristband for your toddler that

simply states: 'If found, please return to any Mother Nature Heavy Industries Service Centre'. Once we are in possession of your toddler we will contact you to arrange collection.

In extreme cases MNHI recommends a leash for absconding toddlers. While tethering your child to yourself or a shopping trolley outside the home may seem a little extreme, MNHI has found this to be the most effective method of controlling toddlers that are prone to running. Make sure you purchase a toddler-specific leash. Leashes designed for canine use may come in nice colours but the use of a choker chain on a toddler is not recommended.

Being the owner of a runner is no fun. You must maintain a state of constant hyper-vigilance, somewhat like being an air-traffic controller, just with more responsibility and drinking. Even at night you must remain alert and put the house in full lockdown in anticipation of an attempted escape, because should there be a breakout it will be you who gets the blame from the co-owner.

The Naughty Words

The first time your toddler swears it will seem cute although surprising. Whether this particular bad habit continues will depend entirely upon how you react to it. If you laugh, your toddler is programmed to take that as encouragement and the potty-mouth antics will continue. Remember, toddlers are designed to be

great mimics and in their thirst for new words, they seem especially attracted to those that are socially unacceptable or relate to bodily functions.

Parents like to believe that all the bad language their toddler spouts forth with has been picked up at creche or from another source other than the home. MNHI advises this is not always the case and that all owners should be particularly vigilant in their everyday lives when they are around their toddler and something goes wrong. It is all too easy to let fly with an expletive when you are cut off in traffic, or you drop something heavy on your toe, but be warned: the bad words you use will be the ones your toddler picks up. Of course your toddler will not know what these words mean, all he knows is that by repeating them he gains extra attention from you. MNHI suggests a softly-softly approach to a swearing toddler; don't go off the handle at him as this will only encourage him to say it again, and again, and again! Remain calm and explain to your toddler that it is not a very nice word and that you don't want to hear it again. Should this method fail, the best you can do is to steer him towards a career in stand-up comedy.

Section E:
Entertainment and Beyond the Home

Now that your toddler is active and preparing to fully activate the speech function, it is time to look at how you will keep him entertained when you are not able to give him your full attention. MNHI manufactures and sells a range of toys and educational aids all designed to keep your inquisitive toddler active and informed.

Toys

As your toddler's brain module grows and flourishes it will need stimulation to help it along the way. The first step towards this is to improve your toddler's fine motor skills. As your toddler learns to pick things up and move them around, something occurs within the brain. MNHI calls it the special reasoning response. Improving on this is a vital part of your toddler's development. There are certain MNHI-approved toys and games for the development of fine motor skills. It is important to remember though, that fun should be the first priority whenever it comes to toys.

At just over 12 months your toddler should be quite adept at banging things together (MNHI suggests a wooden spoon and a saucepan). Although this is annoying from a sound perspective, it is important to note that it is teaching vital hand-eye coordination skills, plus for the budget conscious it is a cheap toy. Also around this time your toddler should begin to use

a crayon to scribble, move objects around the floor and be able to turn the pages of a book. To really help with hand-eye coordination in the early stages, MNHI suggests heading outside and blowing bubbles and watching while your toddler claps his hands and tries to catch them. MNHI recommends you tie up the dog while you play this game to prevent any accidental nips.

At about 18 months building with blocks may become your toddler's favourite activity. This activity starts out with just being able to stack one block on top of another, which will soon lead to three or four block stacks and then every toddler's favourite part; knocking the blocks over. Soon physical coordination will improve and your toddler will be trying different puzzles and stacking up to six blocks at a time, as well as scribbling and painting and taking larger toys apart and putting them back together again. Please note that any toys that are meant for taking apart and reassembling should not contain small pieces because at this age the toddler's first point of exploration is still to put everything in his mouth.

MNHI installs an imagination module in every one of its toddlers. It is up to you as the owner to help develop and nurture this module in your child. Give your toddler the type of toys that will inspire imaginative play (a full range of which is available at all MNHI service centres). Stuffed and plastic animals, dolls and play people that can't be swallowed, cars, planes and trucks all encourage imaginative play. Other things include a toy kitchen and dining set, a play telephone,

a shopping cart and plastic groceries, as well as costumes and dress-up sets.

It is crucial here to point out that any toy being considered for your toddler meets all the relevant safety standards in terms of choking hazards and jamming things in various orifices (a complete list of which is available on our website). While MNHI service centres can dislodge articles stuck in your toddler's throat, we do point out that removing them is both uncomfortable and expensive. Prevention is better than cure in this regard.

MNHI designs every toddler with an inbuilt musician or dancer that is just waiting to present itself to the world. So don't be afraid (or perhaps do be afraid) to bring out the drums and tambourines, the plastic horns and xylophones, even simple keyboards, and let them go nuts. They will play and dance to their heart's content, all the while expressing their creativity and giving you something to record on your camera. Do not be alarmed if your boy toddler shows a preference to dressing up in the girl costumes and dancing to the music, it is preferable to having him constantly playing with himself (see previous section).

The key to buying toys for a toddler is that they need not be expensive. Give a toddler an expensive plaything and it will be broken in no time. Remember, this is not the child's fault. Expensive toys break easily. Toddlers don't need the latest, greatest, most expensive toy on the market; their imagination will enable them to make the most out of whatever they are presented with.

Toys should have an educational component to them as well, and MNHI recommends games that encourage rudimentary numeracy and literacy skills. Blocks with letters and numbers serve as the perfect introduction to the worlds of numeracy and literacy. There are also any number of expensive battery-operated reading aids on the market today; not only will these toys help your toddler with reading but often they will imbue him with basic computer skills. Be warned, the average parents will spend as much money on batteries in the first five years of their child's life as they will on food.

Television

Television is a vital part of any toddler's life and MNHI has designed its toddlers to be able to absorb plenty of it. Determining the type and frequency of the programming your toddler watches is up to you as the owner. Having said that, MNHI makes the following recommendations to ensure that your toddler's television experience is both enjoyable and educational. Shows that include a musical component with songs

that are easy to singalong to are always popular, as are programs with characters dressed in brightly coloured costumes. It is important that your toddler learns something from his television watching experience, so don't just sit him down in front of infomercials (your toddler does not need to know the benefits of the ab roller) and leave him to it. MNHI has a wide variety of educational DVDs for sale online or through its service centres that will entertain and educate the fussiest of toddlers.

Socialisation

MNHI freely acknowledges the demands placed on modern-day parents. That's why we understand that at some stage during the toddler years you may have to relinquish control of your toddler. All our toddlers

have been carefully designed to be able to cope with the rigors of child care (some better than others). As parents return to work after the initial stages of child ownership, it is important to find a good, reliable creche in which to place your toddler.

MNHI advises all of its toddlers are suitable for child care or creche from 12 months of age. Additionally, MNHI is proud to announce that we have opened a string of creches in all capital cities. Our creches are ideally suited to attend to the needs of your toddler on a daily basis, with all meals provided as well as a safe, clean and educational environment in which your toddler will thrive. After all, we designed and built your toddler, so it stands to reason that we know best how to care for him. Should you be interested in enrolling your toddler in a MNHI creche, please contact your nearest service centre or fill out an application online.

It is important for the long-term development and efficiency of your toddler that he be exposed to other toddlers as often as possible. It will not only help develop his social skills but also expose him to common illnesses and help build up his immunity. For these reasons MNHI recommends your toddler joins a playgroup. These groups for toddler owners meet on a regular basis to discuss toddler development as well as football and to play some poker. These groups fulfil a crucial role in toddler ownership in allowing fathers to exchange tips on discipline as well as compare toddler performance. A list of all

MNHI-approved toddler playgroups is available from your nearest MNHI service centre.

MNHI wishes you all the best with your toddler and we are confident that as he grows and develops that you, like the millions of satisfied MNHI fathers before you, will derive great pleasure and pride from your Mother Nature Heavy Industry toddler.

Further reading and resources

Being the father of a toddler can be demanding, as there are ongoing problems and situations that seem to arise on a regular basis. For this reason MNHI has published several books that expand on the information already presented in this manual. All of these books are available for purchase from the accessories department of your nearest MNHI service centre.

Chewing on More than food, Elana Shwartz, 1996

My Friend the Sippy Cup, Jonathon Issacs, 2011

Tantrum Recovery for Beginners, Kerri Freeman, 2002

My Child the Escape Artist, Dr Tim Smith, 1999

Everything Goes Up His Nose, Adam Grundman, 2005

At Bedtime My Nightmare Begins, Dr Nikki Leffko, 2010

Sibling Warfare: It's Not All Bad, Lindy Barda, 1998

Potty Fear and Toilet Nightmares, Mandy Engel, 2004

Thrown Cutlery: How to Avoid Injury, Yaal Broshi, 2009

It Will Work its Way Out: A Guide to Swallowed Foreign Objects, Michelle Ostrow, 2002

The Wiggles Are Evil, Joel Pearlman, 2003

Dogs Are Not for Riding, Aaron Zuckerman, 2008

Appendix
Service history

Keeping track of the servicing and maintenance of your toddler is vital for the long-term ownership experience. In recognition of this, MNHI provides you with this detailed service record so that you may ensure the smooth and efficient running of your toddler. It should also be noted that, should you ever decide to trade in your toddler, these records will ensure you achieve a premium over less well-documented children.

Service history

First toddler service (1 year) — discuss and
record date of first anniversary and first steps:

Service history

Second toddler service — (2 years) general
inspection of body parts:

Service history

Third toddler service (30 months) — analysis
of tantrum and biting history, and general
bad habits:

Service history

Fourth toddler service (3 years) — full review
of word vocabulary and assessment of
good behaviour:

Service history

Service history

Service history

Service history

Service history

Service history

Service history

Service history

Service history

Service history

Baby Owner's Manual

ISBN 9781921878428

RRP AUD $19.99

Perfect gift book for fathers and fathers-to-be

A humorous operating guide for fathers, *Baby Owner's Manual* is sure to bring a smile to any dad's face. Written by a man for men, this book likens a new baby to the other love in a man's life: no, not his wife, his car!

This essential handbook covers everything from delivery of baby from Mother Nature Heavy Industries, regular servicing of your baby, standard equipment, the cooling system and liquid waste disposal, warning signs, even optimising economy and getting the most out of your baby. This is a must-have book for any father-to-be.

Available in all good bookstores or online at www.rockpoolpublishing.com.au